Your Amazing Itty Bitty™

90-Day Breakthrough

15 Action Steps to Overcome Your Fears and Live Your Best Life

Scott Lehmann

Published by Itty Bitty™ Publishing
A subsidiary of S & P Productions, Inc.

Copyright © 2024 Scott Lehmann

All rights reserved. No part of this book may be reproduced or transmitted in any form or by any means, electronic or mechanical, including photocopying, recording, or by any information storage and retrieval system, without written permission of the publisher, except for the inclusion of brief quotations in a review.

Printed in the United States of America

Itty Bitty Publishing
311 Main Street, Suite D
El Segundo, CA 90245
(310) 640-8885

ISBN: 978-1-7322946-4-6

Your Amazing Itty Bitty™ 90-Day Breakthrough

15 Action Steps to Overcome Your Fears and Live Your Best life

Are you ready to unleash the power within you and embark on an exhilarating journey of self-discovery and empowerment? It's time to break free from the limitations holding you back, embrace transformation, and unleash your true potential.

In this book, Scott Lehmann will guide you through 15 practical steps over 90 days to conquer your fears and unleash the incredible possibilities within you.

You will learn to:

- Understand and release your fears
- Create an action plan
- Step out of your comfort zone
- Take inspired action
- And so much more

It's time to seize your power and make your dreams a reality. Get your hands on a copy of this Itty Bitty™ book today and start taking charge of your life!

Dedication

This book is dedicated to the mentors and coaches who have gone before and showed me how to live a better life by teaching me to embrace my fears and experience everything life has to offer.

I also thank my family, especially my wife Jean, for their unwavering support and belief in me.

Stop by our Itty Bitty™ website for exciting blog entries about breaking through your fears and living your best life.

www.IttyBittyPublishing.com

For a companion workbook, videos, and additional resources that help you complete each week's action steps, go to:

www.scottlehmann.com/breakthrough/

Or visit Scott Lehmann's website for more resources to facilitate your growth.

www.scottlehmann.com

Table of Contents

Introduction
Step 1. Understanding Fear
Step 2. Identifying Your Fears
Step 3. Setting Your Intentions
Step 4. Creating an Action Plan
Step 5. Adopting a Positive Mindset
Step 6. Cultivating Self-Confidence
Step 7. Nurturing Self-Care
Step 8. Stepping Out of Your Comfort Zone
Step 9. Facing Your Fears Head-on
Step 10. Building a Support System
Step 11. Embracing Failure as a Learning Opportunity
Step 12. Cultivating Resilience
Step 13. Embracing Vulnerability
Step 14. Taking Inspired Action
Step 15. Maintaining Your Breakthrough

Introduction

Welcome to *90-Day Breakthrough: 15 Action Steps to Overcome Your Fears and Live Your Best Life.* In this book, you will embark on a journey of self-discovery and empowerment. You will explore the power of fear in your life and how it holds you back from reaching your full potential. Get ready to break free from limitations and unlock the greatness within you.

Are you ready to transform your life in just 90 days? You will discover proven strategies to conquer your fears and unlock your true potential. Through practical insights and a step-by-step methodology, this book will ignite your passion, empower you to act and guide you toward living the life you've always imagined.

Read the whole book, internalize its concepts, and then focus on one step each week. If you follow this plan and focus on the action steps, you will build a foundation that will support you to step outside your comfort zone and take risks that will support you in attaining your wildest dreams!

The free companion workbook and videos available at *scottlehmann.com/breakthrough* will facilitate your transformation and assist you in making the changes you know you need to make in your life.

Let's dive in and create the life you've always dreamed of.

Step 1
Understanding Fear

Fear, a universal human emotion, has the power to shape your life and hold you back. Like an invisible barrier, fear restricts you from taking risks, pursuing your dreams, and embracing new opportunities. Fear can limit your life options, causing you to miss countless opportunities. But within fear lies the incredible potential for transformation.

If you want to enjoy all that life has to offer, you must learn to embrace your fears.

1. Understanding your fears empowers you to confront and overcome them. By understanding the root causes and triggers of fear, you can develop effective strategies to face and conquer them head-on.
2. It allows you to cultivate self-awareness and gain insights into your motivations and behaviors. Self-awareness helps you make conscious choices and ensures that your decisions align with your values and goals, leading to a more fulfilling life.
3. It also enables you to empathize with others facing similar challenges. Empathy allows you to offer support and guidance, fostering meaningful connections and building relationships.

More About Understanding Fear

- Fear keeps you in the realm of comfort, shielding you from the unfamiliar and limiting your growth.
- Fear convinces you that failure is inevitable, deterring you from taking risks and pursuing your dreams.
- Fear feeds on self-doubt, whispering in your ear that you are incapable or not deserving of success.

But here's the truth: fear is merely an illusion. By embracing discomfort, embracing failure as an opportunity for growth, and cultivating self-belief, you can break free from fear's grasp and unlock the extraordinary life that awaits you.

Action Steps

- Reflect on the moments when fear's grip was particularly tight and examine how it impacted your decisions and actions. Look at what fear stopped you from doing and the missed opportunities.
- Feel the feelings that stopped you. What were they trying to tell you? Are you willing to confront them for a better life?
- Remember, you have the power to take charge of your life and rewrite your story. Write down the fears that held you back and the situations that provoked them.

Step 2
Identifying Your Fears

As you embark on your thrilling journey of self-discovery, you must peel back the layers, examining the deep-rooted beliefs that have held you back. As you confront these obstacles head-on, be aware that fear may creep in and try to stop you from deeply looking at the patterns of fear that have controlled you.

Be brave and dig deep. Reliving experiences may be painful, but it's a necessary part of this process.

The Fears That Have Controlled You

Let's explore three common fears that control and prevent you from living your best life.

1. Fear of failure: This common fear can paralyze you, holding you back from taking risks and pursuing your dreams with unwavering conviction.
2. Fear of rejection: It stifles your growth, preventing you from embracing new opportunities and forming deep connections.
3. Fear of change: This insidious fear keeps you confined in your comfort zone, inhibiting personal and professional development.

More About Identifying Your Fears

- Review past experiences and reflect on the moments that left you feeling uneasy or anxious.
- Pay attention to your physical and emotional reactions in different situations. Notice the sensations in your body and the thoughts that arise when faced with specific challenges.
- Listen to your inner voice. What thoughts and beliefs consistently emerge when you think about pursuing your dreams or stepping out of your comfort zone?

Action Steps

- An effective exercise to uncover your fears is to gather pen and paper and engage in fearless introspection. Start by creating a list of areas in your life where you feel stuck or avoid taking action. Dig deep into the underlying reasons for your hesitation.
- Ask yourself probing questions, such as "What am I afraid of in this situation?". Allow yourself to be completely honest and vulnerable during this exercise. By facing your fears head-on, you empower yourself to take the necessary steps to overcome them.
- Who would you have to become to reach your goals? Who do you want to be?

Step 3
Setting Your Intentions

Setting intentions is the catalyst for transforming dreams into reality, igniting a fire within you that propels you toward unprecedented success. Intentions carve vital paths toward fulfillment by crysstallizing your desires, focusing your energy, and magnifying your determination.

By consciously aligning your intentions with your intended outcome, you take a massive step in the pursuit of greatness.

Why Intentions Are Important

Following are the three most compelling reasons why setting intentions is crucial to your journey:

1. Clarity and focus: By setting your intention, you gain crystal-clear clarity about what you truly desire in life.
2. Empowerment: Setting intentions empowers you to take control of your life and your destiny. What you focus on in life expands.
3. Overcoming fear and limitation: When you set clear intentions, you confront fear head-on and transform it into a stepping stone for growth.

How to Set Intentions

- Determine what you truly want and why it matters to you. Reflect on your values, passions and dreams to align your intentions with your authentic self.
- Write down your intentions, making them specific, measurable, and achievable. This clarifies your goals, keeps you accountable, and tracks your progress.
- Visualize yourself already living your intended life and feel the emotions associated with it. This practice trains you to believe in your intentions and primes you to take inspired action toward your breakthrough.

Action Steps

- Once clear about your intentions, write them down in vivid detail. The more detail the better, which adds focus to your life.
- Feel the emotions you would feel when you have achieved your goals. Focus on the present moment, not the future or the past.
- Watch for opportunities that appear and take inspired action. Break your intentions into smaller steps and commit to consistent, focused action.

Step 4
Creating an Action Plan

This step explores the crucial process of turning your aspirations into reality. Without a clear structured plan, it's easy to get stuck in a cycle of fear, doubt, and overwhelm.

Creating a strategic action plan allows you to confidently and purposefully navigate the uncertain waters of fear. It empowers you to take ownership of your life and make changes to jump-start your success.

Three Reasons Why Strategic Planning Is Crucial

1. An action plan provides a clear roadmap to reach your goals and helps you break them down into manageable steps while also ensuring focus and direction.
2. Setting specific deadlines and milestones instills a sense of urgency and accountability, propelling you forward with unwavering determination and a built-in action plan with priorities.
3. An action plan acts as a compass to keep you on track and motivated, reminding you of your why, and fueling your passion every step of the way.

How to Create Your Action Plan

- Be specific and define your goals clearly. This will build a strong foundation.
- Break down your goals into smaller, actionable steps. Setting bite-sized tasks gives you a sense of progress and accomplishment, spurring you onward.
- Establish a timeline with specific deadlines. This creates a sense of urgency and keeps you accountable toward your goals.
- Don't forget to celebrate milestones along the way. Rewarding yourself for each accomplishment boosts motivation and reinforces positive habits.

Action Steps

- Reflect on what truly matters to you and what you want to achieve. Be specific, concise, and paint a vivid picture of what success looks like for you. Make sure you create specific actionable goals.
- Next, break down these goals into actionable steps. Identify the specific actions you need to take to move closer to your dreams by setting realistic achievable milestones.
- Finally, establish a timeline and deadlines for each step. This instills a sense of urgency and commitment, driving you to maintain consistent action.

Step 5
Adopting a Positive Mindset

This step will unravel the secrets to cultivating an empowered mindset to conquer any challenge that comes your way. You will learn how to embrace positivity and create a life of happiness and possibilities.

Adopting a positive mindset is crucial because it empowers you to navigate life's challenges with resilience and determination.

How a Positive Mindset Benefits You

1. A positive mindset allows you to view setbacks as growth opportunities enabling you to bounce back stronger.
2. Self-belief and self-confidence enable you to pursue goals and dreams without fear of failure.
3. You recognize your potential and your capabilities, overcome self-doubt, and take bold steps.
4. A positive mindset cultivates a sense of gratitude and happiness, fostering stronger relationships and overall well-being.
5. Positive-minded people attract like-minded people and a supportive community.

How to Adopt a Positive Mindset

- Practice daily gratitude by taking a few moments each day to reflect on what you are grateful for. This simple habit shifts your focus toward positivity.
- Challenge negative thoughts by consciously replacing them with positive affirmations. Reframe self-talk toward empowerment and inspiration.
- Surround yourself with positive influences and supportive people who uplift and inspire you.

Action Steps

- Start each day with positive powerful affirmations to rewire your thoughts and beliefs.
- Practice mindfulness and gratitude. Take moments throughout the day to appreciate the present, focusing on the small joys and blessings around you.
- Visualize your goals and dreams as if they have already been achieved. Create vivid images of yourself succeeding, feeling joyful, and living your best life.
- Surround yourself with positivity. Seek out inspiring books, podcasts, or mentors who radiate optimism and resilience.

Step 6
Cultivating Self-Confidence

To achieve your 90-day breakthrough, you must unlock your true potential and unleash the power of self-belief within. This step explores practical strategies and effective techniques to empower you to conquer your fears and step boldly into a life filled with confidence.

Cultivating self-confidence is crucial; it empowers you to embrace challenges and achieve your goals.

Why Work on Your Confidence?

1. A strong sense of self-confidence enables you to step out of your comfort zone and take risks leading to growth and opportunities.
2. Self-confidence allows you to effectively navigate social interactions, build stronger relationships, and enhance your professional network.
3. Self-confidence breeds a positive mindset and self-belief, enabling you to overcome self-doubt and embrace your full potential.
4. Possessing self-confidence boosts your overall well-being and resilience in the face of adversity. This helps reduce the stress of everyday life.

Building Self-Confidence

Cultivating self-confidence requires consistent effort, but the results are worth it.

- Challenge your inner critic by reframing negative thoughts into positive affirmations.
- Remind yourself of past victories and strengths, fueling belief in your capabilities.
- Develop a routine that includes daily affirmations, positive self-talk, and practicing mindfulness.
- Surround yourself with a supportive tribe that uplifts and believes in you.

Action Steps

- Challenge your comfort zone regularly by setting small, achievable goals that push your boundaries.
- Make a list of your skills, strengths, and accomplishments. Add and refer to it daily.
- Adopt a proactive mindset of self-acceptance and self-compassion. Embrace your flaws and imperfections by acknowledging your uniqueness.
- Seek mentors or like-minded individuals who share your aspirations to create a strong network to nourish and encourage your growth.

Step 7
Nurturing Self-Care

To live your best life, you must embark on a journey of self-discovery and learn the art of prioritizing well-being. One example is tending a beautiful garden. Nurturing self-care is essential for your physical, mental, and emotional health.

Self-care is important, so let's dig in and discover its impact on your overall happiness and fulfillment!

Why Nurture Self-Care?

1. Practicing self-care enables you to recharge and rejuvenate. Caring for yourself combats burnout, reduces stress, and increases your energy levels.
2. Self-care cultivates a positive mindset, allowing you to approach challenges with resilience and optimism. Are you beginning to see how this is all interrelated?
3. By prioritizing self-care, you can enhance your relationships with others. Taking care of yourself makes you more likely to radiate love, support, and empathy.
4. Self-care allows you to invest time in activities that nourish your passions, talents, and dreams.

How to Care for Yourself

- Engage in activities like mindful meditation, exercise, journaling, or enjoying a warm bath. This allows you moments of blissful relaxation and rejuvenation.
- Set healthy boundaries and learn to say no when needed. Remember, preserving your energy and protecting your precious time is crucial.
- Seek moments of connection and engagement by spending quality time with those you love who uplift your spirits and inspire you. Life is about more than just work.

Action Steps

- Set a consistent bedtime routine that allows you to unwind and relax before bed. Get the sleep you need to wake up refreshed and ready to take on the day.
- Carve out dedicated daily time for self-care activities that bring you joy and relaxation. Make self-care a non-negotiable part of your routine.
- Practice setting boundaries and saying no when necessary. Protect your time and energy by gracefully declining commitments that don't serve you. This practice alone will create space in your life for the things you want and need to do.

Step 8
Stepping Out of Your Comfort Zone

By challenging the boundaries of familiarity and venturing into uncharted territory, you open doors to astonishing personal growth, untapped potential, and boundless opportunities. It's within the discomfort zone that true transformation occurs.

You'll discover resilience you didn't know you possessed as fear gives way to courage and doubts are replaced by confidence. This step explores practical strategies and actionable steps to help you overcome your fears.

Why This Is an Important Step

1. When you dare to step outside your comfort zone, you open the door to new levels of success and give yourself the chance to experience extraordinary growth opportunities.
2. Live a fulfilled adventurous life: the comfort zone represents a safe and predictable existence but stifles growth and limits experiences. Dare to break out of the mold.
3. Overcome fear and build resilience: Stepping outside your comfort zone is an act of courage that allows you to conquer your fears.

How to Step Outside Your Comfort Zone

Life truly begins at the end of your comfort zone. Step out in faith and watch the magic unfold!

- First, challenge your fears head-on. Face them with unwavering determination and step into the unknown, for it is there that transformation begins.
- Take baby steps toward discomfort. Start small, but don't be afraid to gradually increase the challenge level. Each step forward will build your confidence and propel you toward greatness.
- Embrace new experiences and seize exciting opportunities. Dive into uncharted territory to learn new skills and connect with new and diverse individuals.

Action Steps

- Challenge your fears like a warrior. Identify your deepest fears and confront them head-on, refusing to let them hold you back any longer.
- Take small but purposeful steps that push the boundaries of your comfort zone. Start by trying new activities, exploring different environments, or meeting new people.
- Embrace discomfort as a catalyst for change, reframing setbacks as opportunities for learning and growth.

Step 9
Facing Your Fears Head-on

By facing fear head-on, you will unlock a world of endless possibilities, propel your personal growth, and ultimately live your best life. Challenging your fears is the key to whatever stops you from realizing your true potential.

Facing fear liberates you from its suffocating grip and empowers you to control your destiny. Are you ready to face your fears head-on and release the extraordinary power that lies within you?

Facing Your Fears

1. By confronting your fears head-on, you reclaim the power that fear holds over you, setting yourself free to chase your dreams and unleash your full potential.
2. Facing your fears cultivates resilience and inner strength, enabling you to overcome obstacles and navigate life's challenges with unwavering confidence.
3. Embracing the discomfort that accompanies facing fears, you open the door to personal growth and self-discovery, unlocking a world of limitless possibilities and creating a life filled with fulfillment and joy.

How to Face Your Fears

- Acknowledge your fears with unwavering honesty. Dig deep within yourself, identify the source of your fears, and confront them head-on with courage and determination.
- Reframe your mindset and embrace the belief that your fears are simply stepping stones to growth. Instead of seeing them as obstacles, see them as opportunities for personal development and breakthroughs.
- Take consistent and incremental actions to face your fears. Start with small steps, gradually challenging yourself to push beyond your comfort zone.

Action Steps

- Confront your fears by identifying them specifically. Write them down and visualize yourself facing each fear with confidence.
- Embrace discomfort by consciously deciding to step outside your comfort zone.
- Create a fearless mindset and challenge the negative thoughts and self-doubt that hold you back.
- Take action and break down your fears into manageable steps and tackle them one by one. You will never look back!

Step 10
Building a Support System

Building a robust support system is paramount to achieving personal breakthroughs and living your best life. The impact of having a solid network of individuals who uplift, encourage, and believe in you cannot be overstated. They provide a shoulder to lean on during challenging times, offer invaluable guidance and perspective, and serve as cheerleaders to celebrate your victories.

A support system instills a sense of belonging, boosts your confidence, and empowers you to take on challenges with unwavering resilience.

The Power of Support in Your Life

1. A support system provides encouragement and motivation when facing challenges.
2. Your support system offers different perspectives and valuable advice.
3. A support system offers accountability to keep you on track and motivated to take concrete steps to achieve your goals.
4. Support systems provide a sense of belonging and emotional support. Sharing your journey with your group creates a safe space to express concerns and celebrate your successes.

How to Find Your Tribe

- Seek out shared interests and passions. Look for communities, clubs, or online groups that cater to your areas of interest. This provides common ground for meaningful connections.
- Prioritize quality over quantity. It's better to have a small circle of genuine, trustworthy individuals who genuinely support you than a large group of superficial acquaintances.
- Be proactive in cultivating relationships. Take the initiative to reach out, attend events or social gatherings, and nurture connections through open communication and active participation.

Action Steps

- Identify your needs and values to determine the kind of support you require.
- Identify those currently in your corner: family, friends, mentors. Evaluate the depth and quality of those relationships.
- Expand your network by seeking out new connections. Attend networking events and join organizations aligned with your interests. Nurture your support system by being proactive and communicating with your tribe.

Step 11
Embracing Failure as a Learning Opportunity

By changing your perspective on failure, you open yourself to unparalleled personal growth and development. Instead of viewing failure as an endpoint or as evidence of inadequacy, you learn to see it as a stepping stone toward success. This shift empowers you to take risks, explore new horizons, and push beyond your comfort zone.

Through failure, you gather invaluable lessons, gain resilience, and propel yourself closer to your goals.

Why Shifting Your Mindset is Key

1. Mindset cultivates resilience and perseverance, allowing you to bounce back from setbacks and continue your pursuit of success. Failure becomes a stepping stone rather than a roadblock.
2. Innovation and creativity come alive when failure encourages you to explore alternatives and think outside the box.
3. Embracing failure as a learning opportunity fosters personal growth and self-discovery. You open yourself to new experiences, ideas and perspectives by embracing failure.

How to Embrace Mindset

- Shift your mindset and redefine failure as a stepping stone to growth rather than a deterrent. Reframe failure as a valuable lesson that provides insight and perspective on your path to success.
- Practice self-reflection and analyze the reasons behind the failure. Identify patterns, strengths, and areas for improvement; use these insights to adapt your approach and refine your strategies.
- Actively seek growth opportunities by stepping outside your comfort zone to embrace calculated risks. Embrace the discomfort of uncertainty and leverage failure as a catalyst for personal and professional development.

Action Steps

- Recognize that failure is not a reflection of your worth but a stepping stone to growth and improvement.
- Embrace reflection and take time to honestly analyze your failures. Identify the lessons learned and adjust as needed in the future.
- Take action, fail forward, and learn. Push yourself to try new things, explore different approaches, and venture into unfamiliar yet promising territory.

Step 12
Embracing Vulnerability

By letting go of protective barriers and allowing yourself to be seen, you deepen your connections with others, foster genuine relationships, and experience true emotional growth.

Embracing vulnerability empowers you to tap into your authentic self, unleash your full potential and unlock a world of possibilities. It opens the door to personal growth, deeper connections, and a more fulfilling existence.

Why Vulnerability Matters

1. Vulnerability allows you to form profound and authentic connections with others, fostering meaningful relationships built on trust and empathy.
2. Embracing vulnerability empowers you to acknowledge and confront your fears head-on, overcome challenges and expand your comfort zones.
3. Embracing vulnerability opens new opportunities and experiences, igniting a sense of courage and resilience that propel you closer to living your best and most rewarding life.

How to Embrace Vulnerability

- Acknowledge and accept your emotions without judgment or shame. Allow yourself to feel vulnerable and recognize it as a sign of strength, not weakness.
- Cultivate self-compassion by treating yourself with kindness and understanding when you step out of your comfort zone. Practice positive self-talk, reminding yourself that growth comes through vulnerability.
- Seek support and connection with trusted individuals who value vulnerability. Surround yourself with a supportive network that encourages and uplifts you throughout your journey.

Action Steps

- Start by identifying and acknowledging your fears. Take time to reflect on the areas where you feel most vulnerable and confront them head-on.
- Share your story with trusted individuals. Seek safe supportive spaces to share your experiences, fears, and aspirations.
- Practice self-compassion and self-acceptance. Treat yourself with kindness.
- Push yourself to regularly step out of your comfort zone. Engage in activities that challenge you to practice vulnerability.

Step 13
Cultivating Resilience

By cultivating resilience, you gain inner strength and mental fortitude to bounce back from adversity, overcome obstacles, and persevere toward your goals. If you actively cultivate resilience, you will be better equipped to handle life's ups and downs.

Resilience is a crucial tool to navigate the challenges and setbacks life throws your way, empowering you to face your fears and overcome self-doubt.

Why Cultivate Resilience?

1. Resilience provides the mental strength to rebound from life's challenges, allowing you to overcome setbacks and obstacles with determination and grace.
2. Cultivating resilience instills a sense of confidence and empowerment, enabling you to take risks and step outside your comfort zone where you become the superhero of your own life story.
3. Resilience is a powerful tool for maintaining mental and emotional well-being to help you navigate stress, adversity, and uncertainty with poise and positivity.

How to Cultivate Resilience

- Develop a growth mindset by reframing challenges as opportunities for learning and growth. Embrace setbacks as valuable lessons that fuel personal development and innovation.
- Practice self-care as a foundation for resilience. Engage in activities that promote emotional and physical well-being, such as exercise, meditation, and maintaining healthy relationships.
- Cultivate a support network of trusted individuals who uplift and encourage you during difficult times.

Action Steps

- Focus on being flexible and adaptable by actively seeking new perspectives and being open to change.
- Make self-care one of your highest priorities. When you are stressed or tired, it is hard to take on the day and see everything as a positive.
- Train your mind to find the positives in every situation, and practice gratitude daily.
- Remember that failures are stepping stones to achieving your goals. They are a natural and inevitable part of life.

Step 14
Taking Inspired Action

Are you ready to ignite a fire within that motivates you to step outside your comfort zone and pursue your dreams with unyielding determination? Say goodbye to the stagnation of self-doubt and hesitation and say hello to a life of boundless success and fulfillment.

The moment you embrace inspired action, your life will transform into a breathtaking adventure where every challenge becomes an opportunity, and every dream becomes attainable.

Why Take Inspired Action?

1. Through inspired action, you become an active participant in shaping your destiny rather than a mere bystander in your own life. Allow yourself to seize opportunities that come your way.
2. By embracing inspired action, you open yourself to a world of opportunities and experiences that may have seemed out of reach in the past.
3. Inspired action propels you beyond the confines of fear and doubt, providing the confidence to pursue your dreams with unwavering determination.

Best Practices for Inspired Action

- Listen to your intuition and trust your gut instincts. Your inner voice knows what's best for you; don't ignore it.
- Divide your goals into manageable steps. By taking small actions each day, you'll gradually build momentum and make progress toward achieving your dreams.
- Stay committed and persevere through obstacles or setbacks that come your way. Remember, true breakthrough requires determination and resilience.

Action Steps

- Identify your passions and desires: Reflect on what truly ignites your soul and brings you joy. Visualize your ideal life and set clear goals aligned with your passions.
- Create a clear and actionable plan: Separate your goals into smaller, achievable steps, and create a timeline to hold yourself accountable. Remember, the journey of a thousand miles begins with a single step.
- Cultivate a mindset of positivity and possibility: Surround yourself with positive influences, practice gratitude, and overcome self-doubt by affirming your capabilities.
- Commit to taking consistent action toward your goals.

Step 15
Maintaining Your Breakthrough

Sustaining your breakthrough is crucial in transforming your life and reaping the rewards of your hard work. By staying committed to your goals, you solidify your progress, ensuring that your newfound confidence and success become long-lasting realities to create a ripple effect in all areas of your life. Your courage and achievements inspire those around you, positively impacting relationships, career, and overall well-being.

Are You Going Forward or Backward?

1. By consistently applying effort and nurturing the changes you've made, you solidify your transformation, making it a permanent part of your life and reducing the risk of regressing back to old habits and patterns.
2. Life inevitably presents obstacles, but staying committed to growth you develop the skills and mindsets needed to navigate them with ease and grace.
3. When you maintain your breakthrough, it inspires others around you. Your commitment and success become examples for friends, family, and colleagues.

How to Keep it Going

- Embrace continuous growth and learning. Seek out new knowledge, skills, and experiences to expand your horizons and stay ahead of the curve.
- Commit to a regular review of your goals and progress. Reflect on your achievements, evaluate your strategies, and make necessary adjustments to stay on track.
- Consistently practice self-care and prioritize your well-being. Nurture your physical, mental, and emotional health through activities like exercise, meditation, and meaningful connections.

Action Steps

- Create a routine that supports your goals. Designate specific times for activities that align with your breakthrough. Incorporating these practices into daily life reinforces your progress and maintains a positive mindset.
- Seek support and accountability. Surround yourself with like-minded individuals who uplift and motivate you.
- Embrace a growth mindset. View setbacks as opportunities for growth and learning rather than as failures. Cultivate self-compassion and resilience, adapting to challenges with grace and determination.

You've finished. Before you go…

Post/Share that you finished this book.

Please star rate this book.

Reviews are solid gold to writers. Please take a few minutes to give us some itty bitty feedback.

ABOUT THE AUTHOR

Scott Lehmann, best-selling author, speaker, coach, and trainer with Maxwell Leadership, is uniquely qualified to help you focus on breaking through fear and conquering it. His experience and track record speak volumes about his ability to empower people to overcome their fears and achieve entrepreneurial goals.

With a masterful knack for reinventing himself throughout life, Scott has transitioned from a bankrupt farmer to thriving in the corporate world. This remarkable journey has equipped him with the tenacity and resilience necessary to understand the fear that can hold you back from taking the leap into entrepreneurship.

Having made the leap himself, Scott transformed his career from the corporate world to becoming a sought-after speaker, coach, and trainer. With a deep understanding of the struggles that come with embracing a new path, he has developed effective strategies to help others to fearlessly navigate the unknown territory of entrepreneurship.

Scott's experience teaching seminars and workshops in the corporate world and the non-profit sector demonstrates his commitment to sharing his expertise with others. He possesses a natural talent for connecting with his audience, instilling the confidence needed to conquer their fears and achieve success.

As a seasoned coach, Scott has guided many high achievers from fear to fortune. His remarkable ability to identify and address underlying fear enables him to provide support to empower you to overcome obstacles and reach your full potential.

One of his distinguishing characteristics is his commitment to constant learning and personal growth. Investing over $100,000 in workshops, seminars, and coaching, he has honed his skills to provide the highest level of guidance and support to those seeking to conquer fear and become successful entrepreneurs.

With over 20 years of experience as a leadership coach and trainer, Scott has developed a unique set of tools and strategies to help aspiring entrepreneurs break through fear to build unshakable confidence. His expertise in coaching people to become influential leaders translates to invaluable insights that propel aspiring entrepreneurs to success.

Scott's proven methods and refreshing approach make him the ideal mentor for those eager to break free from fear and embrace the rewards of entrepreneurship.

Ready to take the leap and conquer fear? Join Scott Lehmann on his social media platforms, where he shares valuable insights and inspiration about overcoming fear, embracing challenge, and achieving entrepreneurial success. Learn more at:
www.scottlehmann.com

If you enjoyed this Itty Bitty™ book you might also like…

Your Amazing Itty Bitty Legendary Leadership Academy by Ed Nicholls Jr., M.Ed

Your Amazing Itty Bitty™ Self-Esteem Book by Jade Elizabeth

Your Amazing Itty™ Bitty Self-Care Book by Denise Schickel, Ph.D.

Or any of the many Amazing Itty Bitty™ books available online at www.ittybittypublishing.com

www.ingramcontent.com/pod-product-compliance
Lightning Source LLC
Chambersburg PA
CBHW071313060426
42444CB00034B/2539